Public Transportation

LET'S RIDE THE
SCHOOL BUS!

Winston Garrett

PowerKiDS
press.

New York

Published in 2015 by The Rosen Publishing Group, Inc.
29 East 21st Street, New York, NY 10010

First Edition

Editor: Norman D. Graubart
Photo Research: Katie Stryker
Book Design: Andrew Povolny

Photo Credits: Cover Lonely Planet/Lonely Planet Images/Getty Images; p. 5 Alan Marsh/First Light/Getty Images; p. 6 Yellow Dog Productions/Photodisc/Getty Images; pp. 9, 18 Comstock/Stockbyte/Getty Images; p. 10 Richard Thornton/Shutterstock.com; p. 13 Amy Walters/Thinkstock; p. 14 FPG/Staff/Archive Photos/Getty Images; p. 17 tobkatrina/Shutterstock.com; p. 21 Jaren Jai Wicklund/Shutterstock.com; p. 22 Purestock/Thinkstock.

Publisher's Cataloging Data

Garrett, Winston.
Let's ride the school bus! / by Winston Garrett — first edition.
p. cm. — (Public transportation)
Includes index.
ISBN 978-1-4777-6522-7 (library binding) — ISBN 978-1-4777-6533-3 (pbk.) —
ISBN 978-1-4777-6517-3 (6-pack)
1. School buses — Juvenile literature. 2. School children — Transportation – Juvenile literature. I. Title.
LB2864.W56 2015
371.8–d23

Manufactured in the United States of America

CPSIA Compliance Information: Batch #WS14PK4: For Further Information contact Rosen Publishing, New York, New York at 1-800-237-9932

CONTENTS

Most American kids ride the school bus to school.

School buses also take students home when school is over.

When a school bus stops to let kids out, all cars have to stop, too.

All American school buses have at least one **emergency exit**.

A group of school buses is called a **fleet**.

13

The first school bus was built in England in 1827. Horses pulled it.

All American school buses have been yellow since 1939.

School bus **drivers** drive school buses. New York has more school bus drivers than any other state.

All kinds of students can ride the school bus.

Do you ride the school bus?

WORDS TO KNOW

driver   emergency exit   fleet

WEBSITES

Due to the changing nature of
Internet links, PowerKids Press has
developed an online list of websites
related to the subject of this book. This
site is updated regularly. Please use
this link to access the list:
www.powerkidslinks.com/putr/sbus/

INDEX